LEARN THE VALUE OF

Love

by ELAINE P. GOLEY

Illustrated by Debbie Crocker

ROURKE ENTERPRISES, INC.
VERO BEACH, FL 32964

Library of Congress Cataloging-in-Publication Data

Goley, Elaine P., 1949–
    Learn the value of love.

    Summary: Depicts situations that demonstrate the
meaning and importance of love.
    1. Love—Psychological aspects—Juvenile literature.
[1. Love. 2. Conduct of life] I. Title. II. Title:
Love.
BF575.L8G65   1987   152.4   87-16318
ISBN 0-86592-380-9

Love

Do you know what **love** is?

Love is helping your sister clean her room
before she even asks you to.

Love is eating your vegetables when your mom
asks you to, even if you don't like them.

When your friend feels sad and you hug him to
make him feel better, that's **love.**

Love is helping your little brother learn the colors when you'd rather play a game.

Being quiet because Dad is working at home,
is **love.**

Holding your little brother close when he falls
down and cries, is **love.**

Love is telling the boys down the street not to tease your neighbor's cat.

When you're quiet in class because you know your teacher wants you to be, that's **love.**

16

Love is letting your friend decide what game you will both play.

You show your **love** by obeying your parents when
they tell you not to play near the street—
because they **love** you and don't want you to be hurt.

When you help your neighbor carry her groceries because she can't carry heavy packages, that's **love.**

Love is taking care of your little brother
when he is sick.

When your dad is sick and you give him a hug,
you're showing that you **love** him.

Love is sending valentines to everyone in your class, and your teacher, too.

Baking your mom some of her favorite cookies
on her birthday, is **love.**

Love is giving your grandma the daisy
you picked just for her.

Love is the special feeling of caring about others as well as ourselves.

Love

"Look at my plant," said Kenny. "I think I'll give it to my mom on Mother's Day."

"Good idea," said Mike, "I will too."

Kenny and Mike walked home from school together. They carried their plants very carefully. All of a sudden, Mr. Park's dog, Bozo, ran out from behind the bushes. Bozo jumped up on Kenny and licked his face.

Kenny was so surprised, he dropped his plant. The flowerpot broke and the dirt fell out onto the sidewalk. Bozo stepped on the plant and crushed it.

"What will I do now?" said Kenny sadly. "I don't have a Mother's Day gift."

"My sister and I bought our mom some slippers," said Mike. "Here, take my plant."

How did Mike show **love?**
How do you show **love** to your parents?

Love

Twins Kim and Karen wanted the same things for their birthday—bicycles.

"Happy birthday, girls," said their mom.

"Bikes!" shouted the girls. "Thanks."

"Now remember, girls, our street is not safe for riding bikes," said their dad. "Ride only on the bike path."

After breakfast, Kim and Karen rode their bikes up and down the path.

"This is no fun," said Karen. "I'm going to ride to Jan's house." Then Karen rode across the busy street and around the corner.

Dad was driving home from the store. He saw Karen ride across the street. Dad stopped the car. He rolled down the window.

"Karen, ride back to the house and put away your bike," said her dad. "You can't ride again until you learn to obey the safety rules I gave you."

Why did Karen's dad take away her bike? How do your parents show they **love** you?

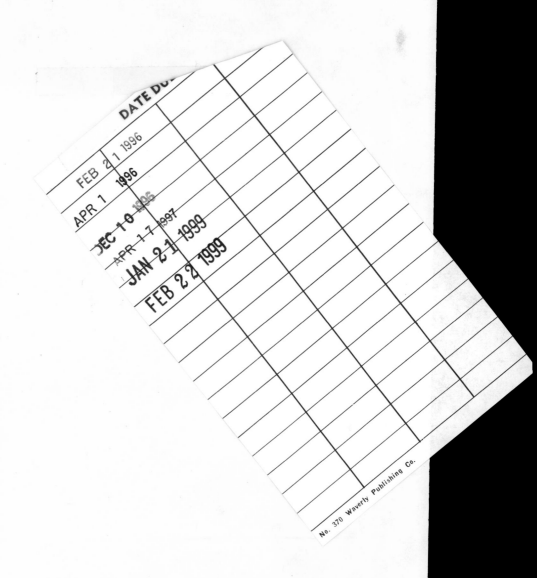